Ukulele for Young Beginners

By Jake Shimabukuro

To access video visit:
www.halleonard.com/mylibrary

"Enter Code"
5400-8955-0829-1063

Cover Photo by Jackson Waldhoff

ISBN 978-1-5400-8087-5

HAL•LEONARD®

Visit Hal Leonard Online at
www.halleonard.com

Contact us:
Hal Leonard
7777 West Bluemound Road
Milwaukee, WI 53213
Email: info@halleonard.com

In Europe, contact:
Hal Leonard Europe Limited
42 Wigmore Street
Marylebone, London, W1U 2RN
Email: info@halleonardeurope.com

In Australia, contact:
Hal Leonard Australia Pty. Ltd.
4 Lentara Court
Cheltenham, Victoria, 3192 Australia
Email: info@halleonard.com.au

Contents

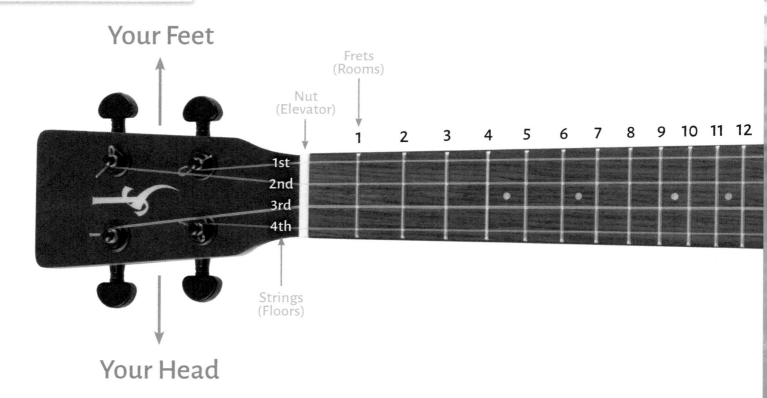

Your Feet

Frets
(Rooms)

Nut
(Elevator)

1 2 3 4 5 6 7 8 9 10 11 12

1st
2nd
3rd
4th

Strings
(Floors)

Your Head

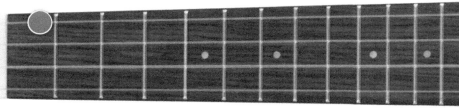

Draw a dot in these "rooms":

(The first one has been done for you.)

First Floor, Room 1

First Floor, Room 3

Second Floor, Room 2

Fourth Floor, Room 1

*Look back at
the previous page
if you need help.*

Pluck the first string with a downward ↓ motion of your right thumb.
This note is called "A."

Don't press any frets.

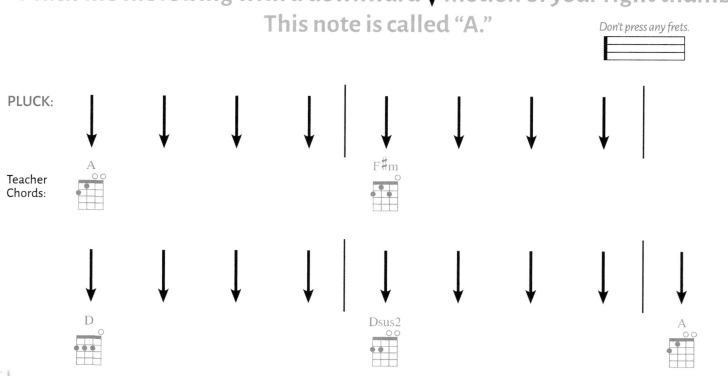

Now, let's pluck the third string! This note is called "C."

(Look on page 2 if you need help finding it.)

Don't press any frets.

PLUCK:

Teacher Chords:

C   Am

F   Fm   C

Plucking any string without pressing a fret is called "open" or "zero."

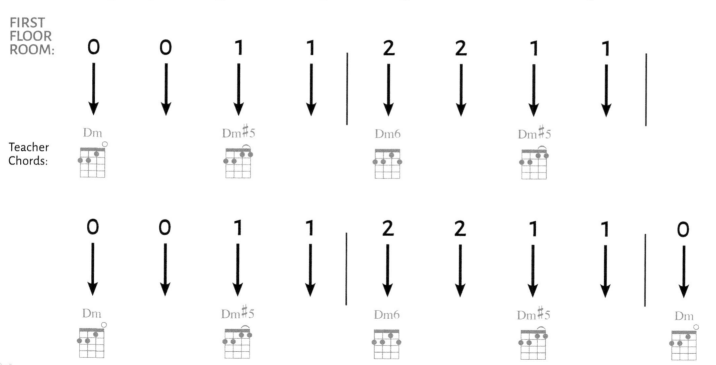

FIRST
FLOOR
ROOM:

0 0 1 1 2 2 1 1

Teacher
Chords:

Dm   Dm#5   Dm6   Dm#5

0 0 1 1 2 2 1 1 0

Dm   Dm#5   Dm6   Dm#5   Dm

Now, let's play a song on the 2nd string!

SECOND
FLOOR
ROOM:

Teacher
Chords:

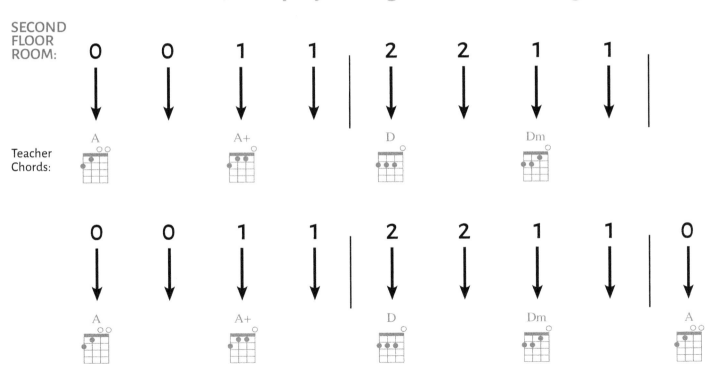

FIRST
FLOOR
ROOM:

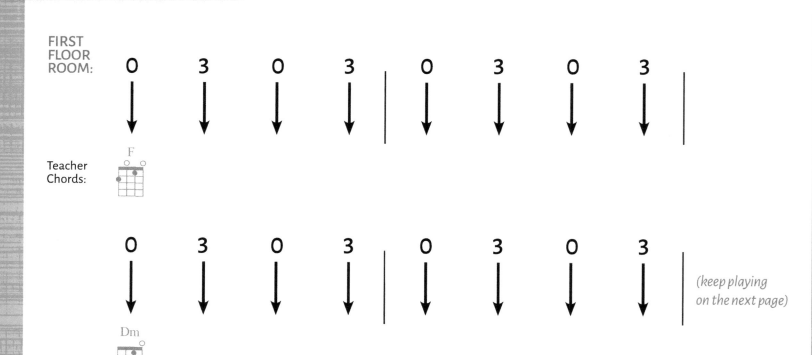

Teacher
Chords:

(keep playing on the next page)

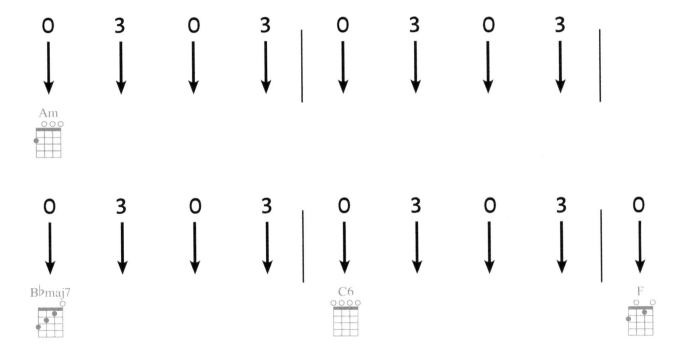

Play these notes from left to right. This is called a major scale.

(Remember the first note is open!)

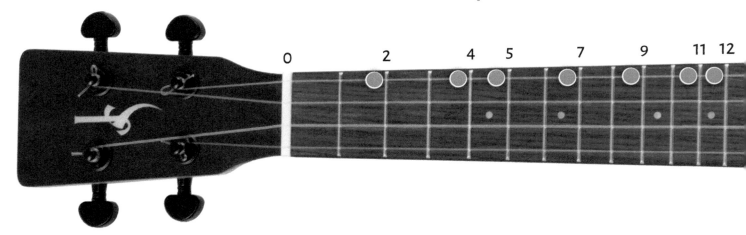

Now you're ready to play a familiar melody.
But first, take a break and complete a word search puzzle.

Circle these words in the puzzle:

FLOOR NOTE

FRET PLAY

FUN ROOM

JAKE SONG

LEARN STRING

MUSIC UKULELE

```
Y  X  F  L  O  O  R  G  H  U
G  L  I  N  F  R  E  T  F  K
Z  E  M  U  S  I  C  P  U  U
J  A  M  O  N  N  Y  L  N  L
A  R  O  O  M  O  M  A  O  E
K  N  V  K  N  T  H  Y  U  L
E  S  O  N  G  E  W  I  D  E
S  T  R  I  N  G  A  Q  R  T
```

Twinkle, Twinkle, Little Star / The Alphabet Song

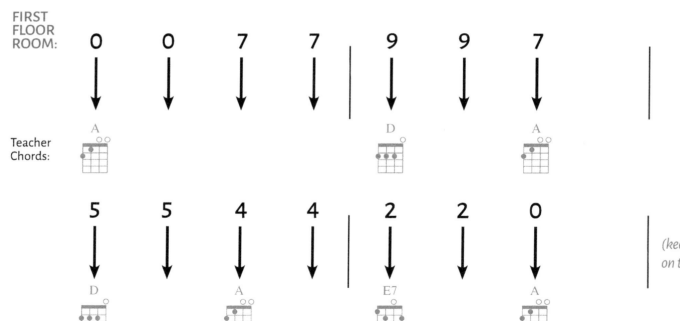

FIRST FLOOR ROOM:

Teacher Chords:

(keep playing on the next page)

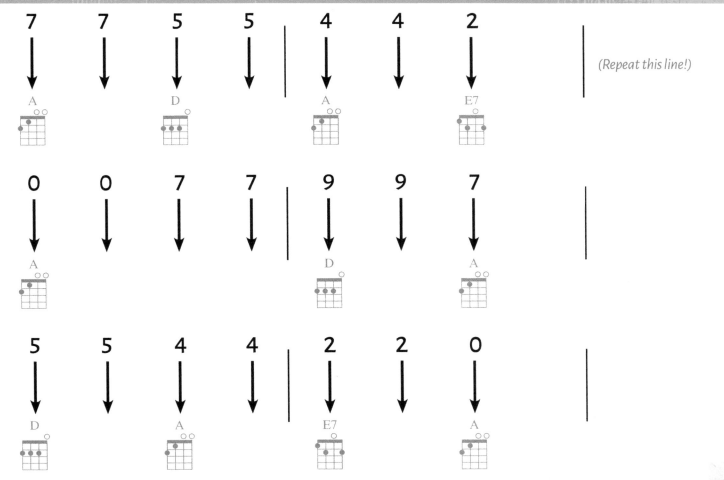

(Repeat this line!)

Row, Row, Row Your Boat

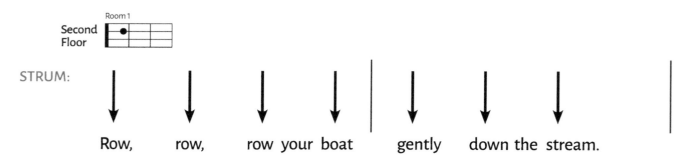

STRUM:

Row,   row,   row your boat | gently   down the stream.

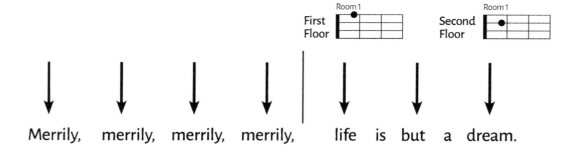

Merrily,   merrily,   merrily,   merrily, | life   is   but   a   dream.

The Incy Wincy Spider

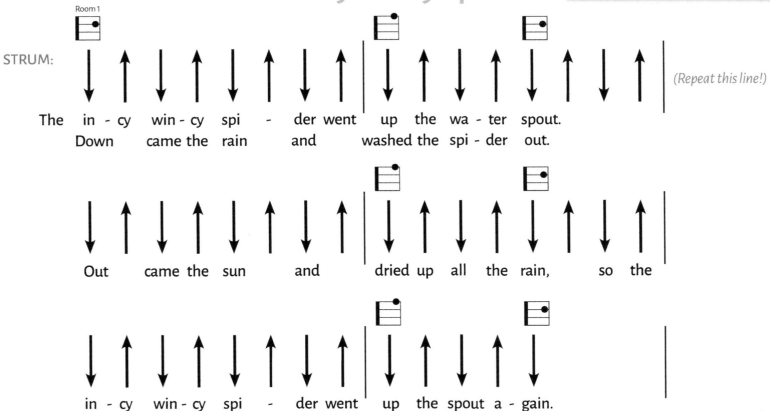

STRUM:

(Repeat this line!)

The in - cy win - cy spi - der went up the wa - ter spout.
Down came the rain and washed the spi - der out.

Out came the sun and dried up all the rain, so the

in - cy win - cy spi - der went up the spout a - gain.

Play these chords over and over.
Your middle finger stays in place the whole time.

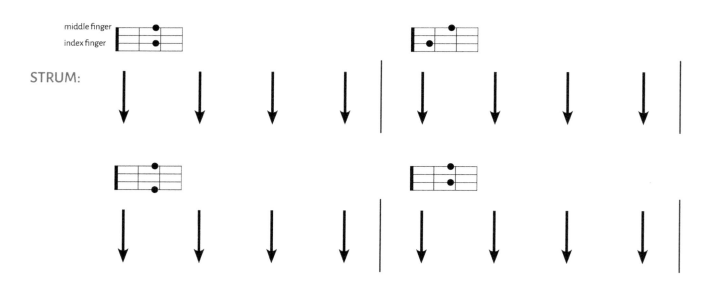

Wow, what a great sound!